Merry Christmas

Alexandra Dannenmann

1st edition: October 2016
Copyright © 2016 Alexandra Dannenmann
Text and illustrations: Alexandra Dannenmann – Stuttgart
Translation: Olga Shimell
www.facebook.com/AlexandraDannenmann.Kinderbuch
www.alexandra-dannenmann.de
ISBN: 978-1539344612

This
book

belongs to:

....

....

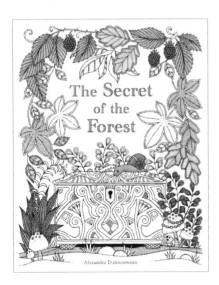

The Secret of the Forest
Search for the hidden pieces of jewellery.

The forest has concealed its secret for many a long year: a splendidly decorated little box buried beneath leaves and mushrooms.
But a wily forest-dweller has discovered the key to the box - and with it the precious jewels inside.
Look for the pieces of jewellery hidden in some of the pictures, and bring the forest to life with vibrant colour.

An enchanting colouring book with over 30 richly detailed hand-drawn illustrations.

Video review: https://youtu.be/fUl83PsXFqc

ISBN: 978-1518833953

The Secret of the Sea
Search for hidden treasure from the sunken ship.

The sea has kept its secret hidden for many years: a sunken ship, loaded with the precious riches of a royal treasure chamber. But storms and raging waves wrecked the ship and sent it plunging to the seabed.

Dive down into the depths of this enchanting water world, past exotic marine dwellers and rare water plants. Look for the treasures concealed in some of the pictures. And bring the underwater world to life with vibrant colour.

An enchanting colouring book with 45 richly detailed hand-drawn illustrations.

Video review: https://youtu.be/vJtIIfy7sv4

ISBN: 978-1530906734

The magic of flowers
Adult Colouring Book: Flowers and Butterflies.

Forget your hectic everyday life with these enchanting floral motifs.

Find your inner peace and balance by colouring in over 30 lovingly hand-drawn illustrations: blossoms, meadows carpeted in flowers, butterflies, floral patterns and mandalas await transformation in the most stunning hues.

Let go of daily life and give free rein to your creativity.

Video review: https://youtu.be/Nthd5WGSWUw

ISBN: 978-1535079631

The Big Grayscale Colouring Book: Mallorca
Colouring book for adults featuring greyscale photos.
Colour, relax and dream of holidays in the sun!

This unique colouring book contains over 45 atmospheric motifs of Mallorca, just waiting to be brought to life with colour.

Each black-and-white photo is child's play to colour thanks to the many shades of grey. Whether you're a beginner or advanced, you'll be able to turn any image into a small work of art.

You'll be thrilled!

Video review: https://youtu.be/eJC__9YqXuA

ISBN: 978-1535079457

Find more information on my homepage http://alexandra-dannenmann.de
or Facebook page http://www.facebook.com/AlexandraDannenmann.Kinderbuch.

Made in the USA
San Bernardino, CA
14 December 2017